USERNAME:
UPRISING

THE RETURN OF THE **SUGG SQUAD**!

MINDY LOPKIN
IS RESPONSIBLE
FOR ALL THE COOL
SPEECH BUBBLES,
EFFECTS AND
LETTERING.

AMRIT BIRDI
IS THE GUY BEHIND
THE INCREDIBLE
ILLUSTRATIONS IN
THE USERNAME
SERIES.

JOE SUGG
CREATED THE
STORYLINE AND
CHARACTERS AND
DIRECTED THE
PROJECT TO MAKE
THE BEST GRAPHIC
NOVEL SERIES
POSSIBLE.

MATT WHYMAN
IS THE PERSON WHO
TOOK THE STORY
AND CREATED A
GRIPPING NARRATIVE
TO ACCOMPANY THE
ARTWORK.

JOAQUIN PEREYRA
BROUGHT THE
IMAGES TO LIFE
WITH HIS AMAZING
COLOURING.

THIS BOOK IS DEDICATED
TO ANYONE WHOSE NAME
ALWAYS AUTOCORRECTS TO
SOMETHING ELSE.

USERNAME:
UPRISING

JOE SUGG

HODDER &
STOUGHTON

First published in Great Britain in 2017 by
Hodder & Stoughton
An Hachette UK company

1

Copyright © Joe Sugg, 2017

With thanks to Matt Whyman
Artwork produced by Amrit Birdi & Co
Illustrator: Amrit Birdi
Colours: Jaoquin Pereyra
Letters: Mindy Lopkin
Ink assists: David Fox

CIP catalogue record for this title is available from the British Library

Hardback ISBN 9781473663312
Trade paperback ISBN 9781473663329
Ebook ISBN 9781473663305

Printed and bound by in Italy by Graphicom srl

Carmelite House
50 Victoria Embankment
London EC4Y 0DZ

www.hodder.co.uk

WELL GUYS, THIS IS IT...

IT'S SO SURREAL TO BE SITTING DOWN AND WRITING THESE WORDS: THIS IS THE THIRD AND FINAL BOOK IN THE USERNAME SERIES. ARGH.

WOW. IT HONESTLY FEELS LIKE YESTERDAY THAT I WAS INTRODUCING THE FIRST ONE! BUT IN REALITY THAT WAS BACK IN 2015... AND WHAT A JOURNEY IT'S BEEN SINCE THEN.

I NEVER COULD HAVE KNOWN BACK THEN JUST HOW FAR THESE BOOKS WOULD COME AND HOW MANY OF YOU WOULD READ AND LOVE THEM. THE AMAZING SUPPORT FROM YOU GUYS HAS MEANT THAT I'VE BEEN ABLE TO REALISE A DREAM OF MINE AND CREATE A GRAPHIC NOVEL SERIES THAT ONCE UPON A TIME ONLY EXISTED IN MY HEAD. THIS SERIES HAS BEEN REALLY SPECIAL TO ME AND I'VE PUT SO MUCH TIME AND WORK INTO IT FROM DAY ONE THAT TO SEE IT GO FROM STRENGTH TO STRENGTH IS EVERYTHING I COULD HAVE HOPED FOR. I'VE SAID IT BEFORE BUT I'LL SAY IT AGAIN, SEEING YOU ALL GETTING INTO THE GRAPHIC NOVEL FORMAT EVEN IF YOU'VE NEVER THOUGHT TO TRY ONE BEFORE, THAT'S SOMETHING I WILL ALWAYS BE SO PROUD OF.

THIS LAST BOOK HAS BEEN SO FUN TO CREATE (DARE I SAY IT'S MY FAVOURITE YET? WAIT, THAT'S LIKE PICKING BETWEEN YOUR CHILDREN ISN'T IT!?), BUT IT'S ALSO BEEN A STRANGE EXPERIENCE BECAUSE WE HAVE TO SAY GOODBYE TO THESE CHARACTERS FOR NOW – CHARACTERS THAT WE'VE ALL BECOME REALLY ATTACHED TO. IT'S A WEIRD FEELING TO HAVE DREAMT UP PEOPLE, IMAGINED WHOLE LIVES FOR THEM, DECIDED THEIR FATES... AND THEN HAD TO FIND A WAY TO SAY GOODBYE TO THEM. BUT I THINK I'VE DONE THEM PROUD AND I CAN'T WAIT TO SEE WHAT YOU THINK.

THE WHOLE USERNAME EXPERIENCE HAS BEEN AN AMAZING
LEARNING CURVE AND TAUGHT ME SO MUCH ABOUT THE ART OF
STORYTELLING – IT'S NOT ALWAYS BEEN EASY, BUT THAT'S THE
POINT ISN'T IT, YOU OWE IT TO THE CHARACTERS TO WORK HARD AND
DEVELOP THEM AND THEIR STORYLINES. ONCE AGAIN I'VE THROWN
IN A FEW NEW FACES AND SOME DRAMA TO SHAKE THINGS UP A BIT,
BECAUSE IF YOU CAN'T GO ALL OUT FOR THE LAST BOOK WHEN CAN
YOU?

BUT AS THEY SAY: ALL GOOD THINGS HAVE TO COME TO AN END...
AND WHAT AN END THIS IS GOING TO BE! BRACE YOURSELF IS ALL I'M
GOING TO SAY. AND MAYBE GET SOME TISSUES ON HAND TOO*.

BEFORE YOU CRACK OPEN THE PAGES OF *USERNAME: UPRISING*
I JUST WANT TO SAY THAT MY BIGGEST THANKS AS EVER IS TO
EACH AND EVERY ONE OF YOU WHO TAKES TIME OUT OF YOUR DAY TO
WATCH MY VIDEOS, SUPPORT MY LATEST ADVENTURE OR SEND ME A
COMMENT ON SOCIAL MEDIA. I GET TO DO AMAZING THINGS BECAUSE
OF MY AUDIENCE AND I AM FOREVER GRATEFUL FOR THAT.

OK, THE TIME HAS COME TO HAND OVER TO EVIE AND THE GANG FOR
ONE FINAL STAND. IT'S BEEN FUN GUYS, ENJOY!

SEE YOU SOON!

JOE

(*SPOILER)

IMAGINE IF YOU'D KILLED ME JUST THEN.

THE **TROUBLE** YOU'D BE IN.

C... C-CAN'T BREA...

YOU'D FACE JAIL TIME, LOSE YOUR JOB, MAYBE EVEN YOUR FAMILY.

IN SHORT, YOUR LIFE WOULD BE OVER.

INSTEAD, HERE WE ARE. AND IN A MOMENT FROM NOW YOU'RE GONNA WISH YOU HADN'T BRAKED IN TIME...

I'M SORRY ...DON'T HURT ME!

...I'M BEGGING YOU...

⸗SIGH⸗

SQUEEEEEEEEED

THEY SAY YOU SHOULD PICK YOUR BATTLES WISELY.

IF YOU WANT TO WIN THE WAR.

KNOX:
E.SCAPE REBE
TROUBLE

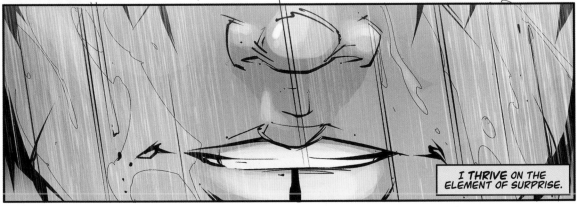

PART ONE

I'M SORRY, ALRIGHT? WHEN I SIGNED US UP I HAD NO IDEA WE'D HAVE SPENT ALL NIGHT BATTLING WITH A GANG OF E.SCAPE OUTLAWS...

... WE SENT THEM PACKING GOOD AND PROPER, THOUGH.

I GUESS THEY TOOK ONE LOOK AT ME AND FIRED UP THE OLD 'BLINK-BLINK' BACK TO E.SCAPE BEFORE I TORE EACH OF THEM A NEW ASS—

IT WASN'T JUST DOWN TO YOU, JASPAR.

WE WORKED TOGETHER WHEN IT MATTERED MOST.

YEAH, THOSE GUYS GOT TOTALLY OWNED, THANKS TO US!

ALRIGHT, SO MAYBE MORE THANKS TO YOU GUYS...

... BUT AT LEAST I TOOK CARE OF EVIE'S LAPTOP.

EVIE, YOUR MUM MIGHT'VE SHUT THE LID ON HER SIDE OF THE PORTAL ONCE SHE ORDERED HER BOYS BACK, BUT YOU NEVER KNOW?

IT'LL STILL WORK FROM HERE IF SHE OPENS IT AGAIN, AND ONE DAY SHE MIGHT CHANGE HER MIND ABOUT THINGS.

LIONEL, MATE ...*LIONEL*... YOU NEED TO, ERM...

OK, IF JASPAR CAN'T SPIT IT OUT, LIONEL, I CAN ... EVIE'S MUM JUST TURNED HER BACK ON HER. DO YOU REALLY THINK SHE WANTS TO HEAR THIS *NOW?*

IT'S OK...

... WE'VE *ALL* BEEN THROUGH A GREAT DEAL. MUM MADE A DIFFICULT DECISION BUT I HAVE TO RESPECT HER FOR IT.

I'M HOPING MAYBE YOU GUYS CAN HELP TAKE MY MIND OFF THINGS.

BY MOPPING FLOORS FIRST THING IN THE MORNING?

C'MON! RIGHT NOW, I SHOULD BE CHILLING OUT AT MALLORY'S WHILE SHE FIXES ME SOME BREAKFAST.

WHAT?!?

LATER...

I CAN'T BELIEVE JASPAR COULD DO THAT TO ME, EVIE!

TO BE FAIR, IT WAS YOU WHO DUMPED HIM.

YEAH, BUT HE DIDN'T STOP ME! AND NOW IF FEEL LIKE MY HEART JUST SNAPPED IN TWO!

DON'T TAKE THIS THE WRONG WAY, BUT THERE MUST'VE BEEN TENSION BETWEEN YOU TO BREAK UP OVER SOMETHING AS TRIVIAL AS EGGS.

IT SOUNDS LIKE IT WAS BOUND TO HAPPEN SOONER OR LATER.

I CAN'T LIVE WITHOUT HIM, EVIE. MY LIFE IS RUINED!

LATER...

TAKE A DEEP BREATH, MAL. YOU WERE DISTRAUGHT A MOMENT AGO, AND NOW YOU'RE ALL FIRED UP.

CALM DOWN?

CALM DOWN!

CALM DOWN?

SWISH

AFTER WHAT HE'S DONE? I'M SO ANGRY!

LATER...

Y'KNOW WHAT, EVIE? YOU'RE RIGHT! JASPAR WAS GETTING ON MY NERVES, BUT I DIDN'T REALISE IT UNTIL TODAY.

I THINK THIS SPLIT COULD BE GOOD FOR ME!

THAT WAS QUICK!

IF MY BROTHERS AND SISTERS BACK HOME COULD SEE ME NOW...

... I HOPE THEY WOULD BE PROUD.

FOR THE GIRL IN MY SIGHTS FOOLISHLY CAST THEM FROM THIS WORLD...

... AND EFFECTIVELY DECLARED WAR.

SO, WHAT HAVE WE MISSED WHILE WE WERE OUT?

PLEASE DON'T TELL ME EVERYONE IS TALKING ABOUT THE BREAK UP OF THE CENTURY...

WELL, ACTUALLY ... NO.

WHAT?! HIT REFRESH!

WHRRRRRRR

THERE ARE LOTS OF PICS AND GOSSIP FROM THE GRAD BALL, BUT MOSTLY IT'S JUST MEMES ABOUT THE NEW PRIME MINISTER AND HIS LATEST APPOINTMENT.

POLITICS? HOW DULL.

ACTUALLY, YOU'LL LAUGH WHEN YOU SEE IT.

NO WAY! SERIOUSLY?

YOU CHOOSE, EVIE. ALIEN SCI-FI, TEEN DRAMA OR STEAMY THRILLER?

AFTER ALL THE CRAZY STUFF THAT'S HAPPENED TO US LATELY...

...HOW ABOUT SOME REALITY TV?

CREEK

HOME.

TIME TO RALLY THE TROOPS.

TAP

TAP

KLIK

KLAK

TAP

BLINK

MEMO

SAFE JOURNEY...

MARK MY WORDS, HE'LL BE PUNISHED WHEN HE DOES BRAVE FACING ME. BY TAKING OUT A BRUTE AFTER I HAD ORDERED YOU ALL TO STAND DOWN, THAT BOY CAUSED MY DAUGHTER AND HER FRIENDS UNDUE PAIN AND SUFFERING.

NOW I KNOW YOU'RE A LIVELY BUNCH. THAT'S WHY I SET RULES SO YOU CAN THRIVE.

I WILL NOT ALLOW ONE BAD APPLE TO UNDERMINE THAT.

BUT --

THAT'S *ENOUGH*, ARLO!

GET ON WITH YOUR TASKS FOR THE DAY!

ARLO, YOU'D BE WISE TO USE THE TIME TO REMIND YOURSELF THAT I WILL *NOT* TOLERATE DISOBEDIENCE.

≶GRUMBLE≶

WHO DOES SHE THINK SHE IS? KNOX COULD BE IN TROUBLE BUT SHE'S MORE CONCERNED WITH MAKING SURE WE PLAY NICE.

WELL, I'M TIRED OF HER TELLING US WHAT TO DO...

IT'S TIME SOMEONE STOOD UP TO HER!

THWOK

HEY, GO EASY!

ARLO. YOU'RE SUPPOSED TO BE CHOPPING LOGS, NOT SPLINTERING THEM INTO MATCHSTICKS!

SHE DOESN'T CARE ABOUT US! IT'S ALL ABOUT MAKING SURE WE DON'T CAUSE TROUBLE.

SO STAND UP TO HER. YOU WOULDN'T BE THE FIRST TO CONSIDER IT. SHE'S BEEN BOSSING US ABOUT FOR TOO LONG NOW.

AND HOW D'YOU SUGGEST I DO THAT?

WITH ENOUGH SUPPORT YOU CAN DO ANYTHING...

... YOU CAN COUNT ON ME, ARLO, AND MANY OTHERS. IT'S TIME FOR FRESH BLOOD ON THE THRONE.

33

OK, LISTEN UP. WHERE ARE MY WORKERS? THEY HAVEN'T REPORTED FOR DUTY YET.

LATER...

I SAID... WHERE ARE MY WORKERS?

CHATTER

CLINK

CHATTER

HA

HA

CHATTER

CLINK

ARLO, CAN YOU HELP OUT HERE. TAKE TWO FRIENDS AND HEAD DOWN TO THE WASH STATION RIGHT AWAY.

CHATTER

CHATTER

HA!

CLINK

≈SNICKER≈

NO.

?!

?!

34

WHAT DID YOU JUST SAY?

NO.

IT'S QUITE SIMPLE. I WON'T FOLLOW ANY MORE ORDERS FROM YOU.

I SUGGEST YOU DON'T PLAY GAMES WITH ME, YOUNG MAN.

REMEMBER YOUR RANK AND LOOK LIVELY.

DIDN'T YOU HEAR ME THE FIRST TIME?

I SAID *NO!*

I WON'T DO WHAT YOU TELL ME ANY LONGER.

AND I SPEAK FOR US ALL!

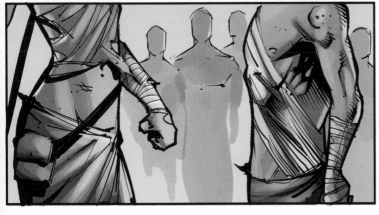

I AM AN ALIEN IN THIS WORLD. EVERYTHING IS STRANGE TO ME.

ZZMMM

AND A LITTLE OVERWHELMING.

ZZZMM

THEIR TECHNOLOGY IS IMPRESSIVE.

WORLDS APART FROM OUR OWN.

BUT THEIR GREATEST STRENGTH IS ALSO A WEAKNESS.

Joe Sugg

The Poop Scoop #3 I AM LIVE

THEY'RE SO LOCKED ONTO THEIR SCREENS AND GADGETS...

... THAT IT SEEMS I CAN MOVE AMONG THEM UNSEEN.

ZZZMMMM

ZZMM

ZMM

IT MEANS THIS WOLF IS NOT SIMPLY OUTSIDE THEIR DOOR.

ZZZMMMMZZZMMM

IT'S ALREADY IN THEIR HOUSE.

ROAMING THROUGH ROOMS.

DRAWN BY THE SCENT OF ITS QUARRY.

LEAVING NO PLACE TO HIDE.

CREAK

WHEN MY BROTHERS AND SISTERS ANSWER MY CALL, THEY WILL SEE FOR THEMSELVES THAT THIS WORLD IS EASY PREY.

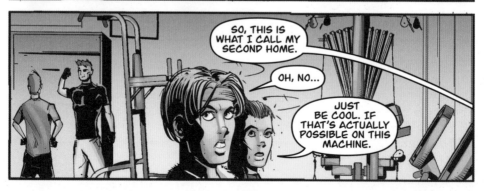

EASY THERE, FELLA.

YOU SHOULD HAVE SOME RESPECT FOR THE WEIGHTS.

ARE YOU HURT?

I'M FINE. TOTALLY COOL. ≥COUGH≥ ≥COUGH≥

JUST NEED A LITTLE AIR, THAT'S ALL. ≥COUGH≥

JASPAR LOOKS LIKE HE'S IN PAIN.

D'YOU MEAN FROM THE ACCIDENT OR THE BREAK-UP? BECAUSE BOTH ARE HURTING HIM RIGHT NOW.

HAS HE TALKED TO YOU ABOUT MALLORY?

OF COURSE NOT. NEVER GOING TO HAPPEN!

OH, YEAH. A GUY THING, RIGHT?

AND HOW ARE YOU DOING? AFTER... EVERYTHING.

ME? FINE! I'M NOT THE ONE DEALING WITH A BREAK-UP HERE.

I MEAN, YOU'VE LOST A LOT RECENTLY. WHAT WITH YOUR MUM TURNING HER BACK ON YOU—

THAT'S NOT HOW I SEE IT.

SHE HAD HER REASONS TO RETURN TO E.SCAPE, JUST AS I HAVE REASONS TO STAY HERE.

WE'RE WORLDS APART NOW, BUT THAT DOESN'T MAKE US ENEMIES.

THE SAME GOES FOR JASPAR AND MALLORY.

THEY MIGHT BE ON SEPARATE PATHS NOW, BUT THAT CAN'T TAKE AWAY FROM THE GOOD TIMES THEY SHARED. IF YOU CAN HOLD ONTO THAT, AND ACCEPT THAT SOMETIMES PEOPLE JUST WANT DIFFERENT THINGS IN LIFE, YOU'LL FACE THE FUTURE FEELING STRONGER FOR THE EXPERIENCE.

YOU SOUND LIKE SOMEONE WHO'S GIVEN THIS SOME THOUGHT.

I JUST HOPE THAT WHEN THINGS CALM DOWN BETWEEN MALLORY AND JASPAR THEY'LL LOOK BACK WITH FOND MEMORIES AND EVEN FIND A WAY OF STAYING FRIENDS. UNTIL THEN...

... I GUESS WE SHOULD ALL JUST LIVE FOR THE MOMENT!

E.SCAPE

OPEN IT. GO ON...

NO WAY!

YOU'RE THE ONE WHO'S WORRIED KNOX NEVER FOLLOWED US THROUGH THE PORTAL.

ANYTHING COULD HAPPEN IF WE LIFT THE LID. YOU DO IT!

HE'S OUR BLOOD BROTHER, AND I REFUSE TO GIVE UP ON HIM.

BUT ARLO, WE WERE FORCED TO LEAVE THAT WORLD IN SHAME... WHAT IF THEY'RE WAITING TO SPRING A REVENGE ATTACK?

STAND BACK...

as she realises what misery she has brought upon her world.

Don't let me down – **KNOX**

By now, you'll be aware that I didn't return to e.scape with you. Instead, I chose to stay behind to settle scores. The girl, Evie, must pay for clipping our wings just as we were set to fly. But in shadowing her, I've come to realise there's a greater prize at stake here... My brothers and sisters, this world is ours for the taking!

No doubt you will ask how a small band of warriors can possibly take on a planet. Having spent time here, I can tell you these people are slaves to their phones and computers, their smart toys and gadgets. It's pitiful to witness such dependence, but if we turn a blind eye I believe such technology could evolve to become a threat to our way of life. We must strike now, while we have the upper hand.

My brothers and sisters, here's what you must do for me to begin this uprising. Firstly...

begin this uprising. Firstly...

... I must ask you to visit our creator's hovel palace. There, you'll ... units that will surely overwhelm you. ... genius, I understand he was meticu- ...ecords. I have every faith that by looking ... uncover instructions that will allow you ... tap into the ... core and redirect it ... will serve ... when we go in ...ce, we send in a ...sign the most f...

Once they have caused panic, mayhem ... four corners of their globe, we ...leas... mass d... you ... cannot ... eyes... shock a... my enemy as she realises what misery ... orld.

Don't l...

Don't let me down - KNOX.

THOSE BOYS WOULD BE WISE TO LEAVE THAT WORLD ALONE...

...AND REMIND THEMSELVES OF THE TROUBLE WE CAUSED BY CROSSING OVER IN THE BLINK OF AN EYE.

I MUST SHOULDER THE BLAME FOR THE LOSS OF ONE OF OUR OWN...

...AND THE PAIN I HAVE CAUSED HIS SOUL MATE.

I EXIST TO WELCOME, GUIDE AND INSPIRE. ONLY NOW IT SEEMS I MUST TAKE ON ONE MORE ROLE...

TO CONSOLE.

RIVER, CAN WE TALK?

I JUST FEEL SO RESPONSIBLE. HAD I NOT DISTRACTED YOUR FRIEND, JUST MOMENTS BEFORE THOSE DEADLY DARTS RAINED DOWN ON HIM, HE MIGHT STILL BE WITH US TODAY.

STOP! JUST STOP THERE.

WE CAN'T CHANGE WHAT HAPPENED, BUT OAK WOULDN'T WANT IT TO COME BETWEEN US.

THAT BRUTE TAUGHT ME NOT TO JUDGE.

PEOPLE SAW HIM AS A MONSTER.

WE BOTH KNOW HE WAS AS GENTLE AS A LAMB.

VERY WELL, FIRST I NEED TO CREATE A NEW GATEWAY TO THE OTHER WORLD. ONE THAT WE CONTROL...

UH HUH.

THEN I NEED TO FIGURE OUT HOW E.SCAPE IS POWERED. THERE MUST BE A PLUG OR SOMETHING.

AH, OK...

WELL GOOD LUCK WITH THAT, ARLO! THERE IS NO PLUG, YOU BUFFOON!

WE'RE TALKING ABOUT PIONEERING TECHNOLOGY CREATED BY A GENIUS WHO WORKED BY HIS OWN RULES. IT'LL TAKE YOU A *LIFETIME* TO FIGURE IT OUT!

BOYS, WE COULD BE HERE FOR SOME TIME.

≈GASP≈

DON'T MOCK ME! YOUR DARLING DAUGHTER IS ALREADY IN BIG TROUBLE FOR DARING TO CROSS US!

LEAVE EVIE OUT OF THIS!

KEEP PLAYING ME FOR A FOOL A I'LL MAKE SURE S SUFFERS MORE TH YOU CAN IMAGIN

AS EVIE'S PARENTS, YOU A THE CREATOR M GO WAY BAC

THAT TELLS ME YOU UNDERSTAN HIM BETTER THA ANYONE ELSE.

THERE HAS TO BE A WAY TO CRACK THE SYSTEM HERE...

... AND YOU'RE THE ONE TO HELP ME!

IF I DO THIS, IT'S FOR EVIE.

BUT IF YOU TARGET MY GIRL IN ANY WAY I'LL--

YEAH, YEAH...

... NOW SHUT UP AND SHOW ME HOW TO MAKE SENSE OF THIS MADHOUSE!

FOR A START, YOU'RE LOOKING IN THE WRONG PLACE. POWER CORE PRODUCTION AND GATEWAY BUILDING ARE CENTRAL TO E.SCAPE'S EXISTENCE, SO THE CREATOR KEPT THOSE MANUALS CLOSE TO HIS 'CONTEMPLATION CHAIR.'

OBVIOUSLY...

UMM... ANY CHANCE YOU CAN GIVE ME A CRASH COURSE?

UNBELIEVABLE! OK, WELL I'M DOING THIS FOR MY DAUGHTER.

LET'S START WITH THE BATTERY CORE. E.SCAPE'S ENGINE ROOM, IF THAT MAKES IT EASIER FOR YOUR PEA-BRAIN TO PROCESS. THE CREATOR COOKED UP A CLEAN, SELF-FUELLING GENERATOR...

... THAT BURNS BRIGHTER THAN ONE HUNDRED SUNS. THE OLD WORLD COULD HAVE LEARNED A LOT FROM HIM.

WHERE IS IT?

RIGHT BENEATH OUR FEET.

THE CORE FUELS EVERY ASPECT OF OUR LIVES HERE. WITHOUT IT, E.SCAPE WOULDN'T EXIST.

EVERYTHING FROM THE ROTATION OF OUR SUN TO THE SWAY OF A GRASS BLADE IN THE BREEZE, IT'S ALL POWERED BY THIS REALM'S BEATING HEART, AND CODED BY ONE VERY CLEVER MAN.

!?!

I EXPECT YOU'D LIKE TO TAKE A CLOSER LOOK.

?!?

Inspection Platform

JUST LIKE YOUR CREATOR, THIS PLACE IS FULL OF SURPRISES.

WHAT THE...?

I'D HAVE FOUND THIS ON MY OWN IF YOU HADN'T DISTRACTED ME.

YEAH, RIGHT.

SLIDE

SLIDE

THE SOURCE OF ALL LIFE FOR E.SCAPE.

IT'S THE HEART OF A VIRTUAL CREATION THAT FEELS AS REAL TO YOU AS IT DOES TO ME--

IT'S REAL!

-- AND FOR THE LITTLE GIRL WHOSE FATHER WAS JUST TRYING TO LOOK OUT FOR HER. E.SCAPE WAS HIS GIFT TO EVIE. A VIRTUAL SANCTUARY SHE COULD VISIT TO GET AWAY FROM IT ALL. SHE MEANT THE WORLD TO HIM.

YEAH, YEAH.. BUT CAN THIS BATTERY CORE BE REPROGRAMMED?

OF COURSE. IF YOU KNOW HOW TO CODE.

LET'S JUST SAY I NEED TO DRAW ON THE POWER FOR SOMETHING... SPECIAL.

THIS WORLD IS A COMPUTER PROGRAMMER'S DREAM, ARLO.

BUT MESSING ABOUT WITH ANY POWER SOURCE NEVER ENDS WELL.

THAT'S WHY YOU'RE GOING TO REPROGRAMME THE CORE WHILE I BUILD MYSELF A GATEWAY.

FOR EVIE'S SAKE, WE'RE A TEAM NOW.

MAYBE I SHOULD JUST FIRE UP THE APP AND HEAD HOME.

KLLIK

OH, NO... PLEASE DON'T SAY I'M STUCK HERE?

BRRK

G'LING

OH, NO! THAT'S MAL WITH EVIE...

... AND EVIE'S LAPTOP...?

65

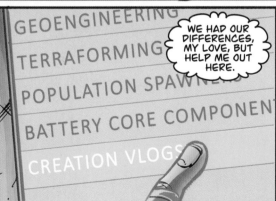

RIGHT. THAT SHOULD BE RECORDING... WHY CAN'T I SEE ME?

OH, WRONG WAY ROUND!

THAT'S BETTER. OK. SO, WELCOME TO MY WORLD... ONE I'M SOON TO LEAVE.

THIS LITTLE OFFICE MIGHT NOT LOOK LIKE MUCH, BUT IT'S HERE THAT I'VE CREATED A DIGITAL REALM.

IN TIME, IT'S ONE OUR SWEET BABY DAUGHTER, EVIE, WILL BE ABLE TO CALL HER OWN.

I CALL IT E.SCAPE! WHERE NOTHING CAN GO WRONG FOR HER. AT LEAST I HOPE IT WON'T!

I'VE GONE TO GREAT LENGTHS TO ENSURE THAT EVERYTHING RUNS SMOOTHLY. AS A FINAL PRECAUTION, IT'S MY DUTY TO RECORD THE STEPS THAT SHOULD BE TAKEN IN AN EMERGENCY.

SO, WHOEVER'S WATCHING THIS -- HI!

I DIDN'T SEE YOU COME IN. HEY, ARE YOU ... CRYING?

NO! MUST HAVE A COFFEE GRAIN IN MY EYE OR SOMETHING.

HAVE YOU BEEN LOOKING AT MY...

OF COURSE NOT! OK, A BIT...

JASPAR, NO GOOD COMES FROM DWELLING ON THE PAST.

I KNOW YOU'RE HURTING ABOUT MALLORY RIGHT NOW...

... BUT IF YOU'RE GOING TO COME TO TERMS WITH WHAT'S HAPPENED, THEN FOCUS ON ALL THE GOOD THINGS YOU HAVE TO OFFER INSTEAD OF WHAT YOU'VE LOST.

SL AM

GOOD THINGS LIKE WHAT? EVIE, I'M LOST WITHOUT HER!

WELL, LET'S SEE...

... YOU'RE ENTERTAINING COMPANY, LOYAL, FUNNY. DO I NEED TO GO ON?

A LITTLE BIT MORE WOULD BE GOOD.

OH, JASPAR! C'MON!

YOU'RE A FRIENDLY GUY WITH LOTS TO OFFER. HOLD ONTO THAT, LEARN TO LIKE YOURSELF AGAIN, AND PEOPLE WILL SOON START PAYING ATTENTION FOR ALL THE RIGHT REASONS.

Y'KNOW, IT HURTS JUST TO THINK ABOUT HER AT THE MOMENT.

IT'S ONLY NATURAL. I'M STILL RAW ABOUT MUM, BUT THERE ARE POSITIVE THINGS GOING ON FOR US BOTH RIGHT NOW.

SCHOOL'S OUT, AND WE CAN COUNT ON GOOD FRIENDS TO HELP US MAKE THE MOST OF IT. THINGS CAN ONLY GET BETTER, JASPAR, BUT YOU HAVE TO WANT TO MAKE THAT HAPPEN.

EVIE, YOU'RE RIGHT. IT'S FINE TO FEEL SAD BUT I NEED TO MOVE ON, AND THAT TIME HAS JUST ARRIVED.

I SHOULD KISS YOU FOR THAT ADVICE, BUT Y'KNOW...

... I DON'T WANT YOU TO FACE THE KIND OF HEARTBREAK I'VE JUST BEEN THROUGH.

PRETTY SURE I'LL SURVIVE, JASPAR, BUT I APPRECIATE THE THOUGHT – EVEN IF IT IS A BIT WEIRD.

74

NOW MAKE SOME ROOM AND PREPARE TO BE IMPRESSED. YOU CAN'T JUST PUSH US AROUND ANY MORE!

ARLO, THIS WORLD IS NOT A WEAPON! THAT'S THE LAST THING THE CREATOR INTENDED!

THE CREATOR IS HISTORY. HE'S DUST NOW!

WE'RE THE FUTURE, SEE? EVEN BETTER THAN THE REAL THING!

GEOF...

TE...

POPULATION SPAWNERS

KLIK

BATTERY CORE COMPONENTS

CREATION VLOGS

LISTEN TO ME, ARLO! E.SCAPE CAN REGENERATE. IT CAN BE UPGRADED, REFITTED AND MODIFIED, BUT THE WORLD IN YOUR SIGHTS ONLY HAS ONE LIFE!

THEN WE SHOULD PUT IT OUT OF ITS MISERY.

HERE WE GO...

BLAM BLAM BLAM BLAM BLAM

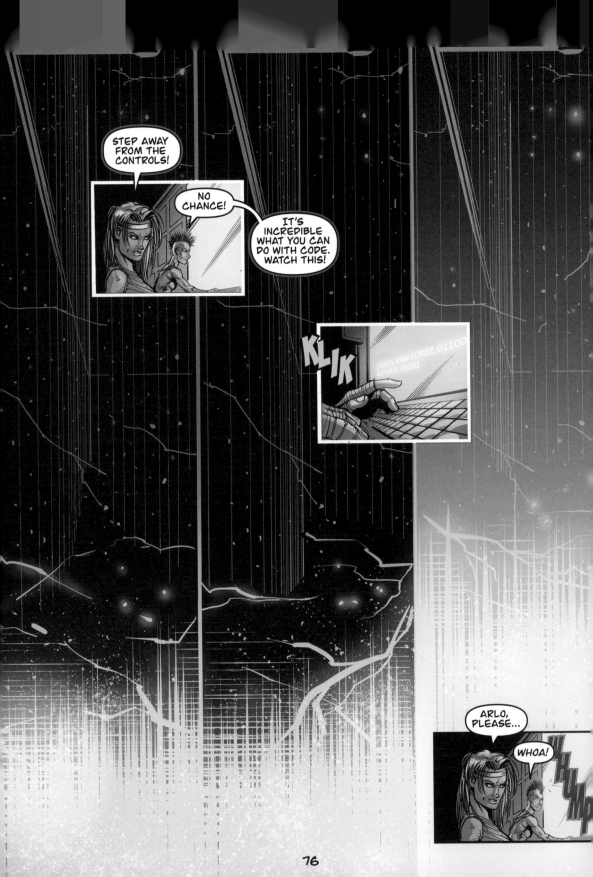

... AND THEN...

... HE HANDED ME A COFFEE WITH CHOCOLATE SPRINKLED ON TOP IN THE SHAPE OF A HEART.

EVIE, I'M LIKE AN ESPRESSO SHOT OF HOTNESS. HE'S CRAZY FOR ME!

AMAZING.

ANYWAY, WHO WAS THAT GUY YOU WERE TALKING TO AS SOON AS I TURNED AROUND?

LOOKED A LOT LIKE JASPAR.

AH, HE HAD PLACES TO GO. JUST LIKE YOU, IT SEEMS.

JASPAR NEEDS TO HEAL, BUT HE'LL GET THERE. WE ALL FIND OURSELVES IN TIME.

SHRIEEEK

D'YOU HEAR THAT?

HOW CAN THAT BE POSSIBLE? MY LAPTOP IS RIGHT HERE WITH ME.

BLINK BLINK

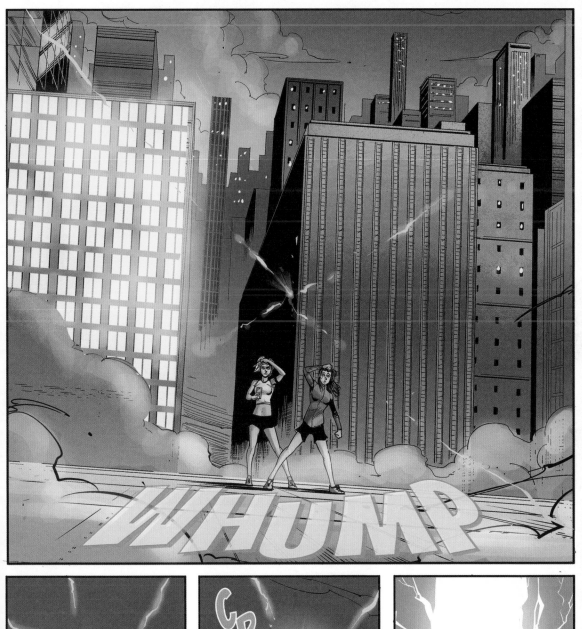

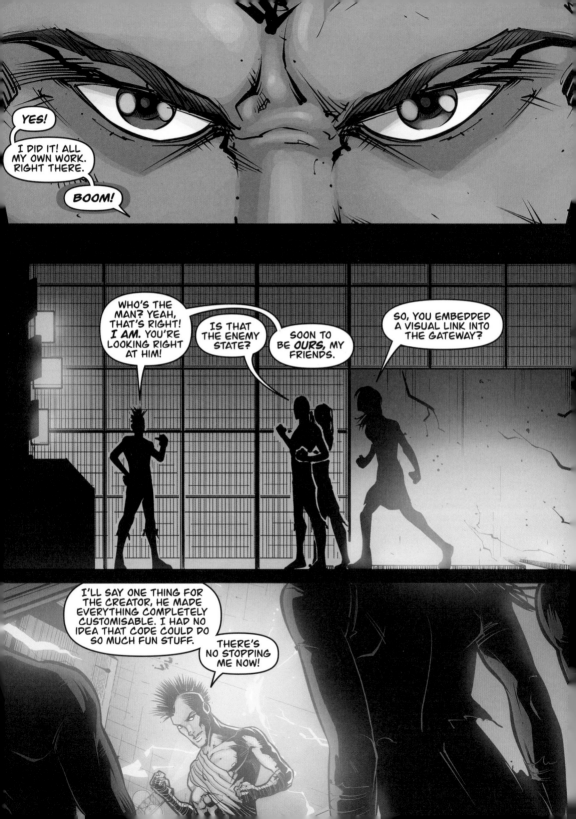

ARLO, THAT POWER CORE IS ON THE CUTTING EDGE OF TECHNOLOGY. ONLY ONE PERSON TRULY UNDERSTOOD ITS CAPABILITY, AND HE'S NO LONGER WITH US.

I BEG YOU TO CLOSE THAT GATEWAY BEFORE THINGS GET OUT OF HAND!

BUT IF I SHUT THAT ONE...

... I'D HAVE TO CLOSE THEM ALL!

YOU MADE *MORE*?

WHAT CAN I SAY?

THE DUPLICATE FUNCTION WAS IRRESISTIBLE.

I THOUGHT I'D SHARE THE MAGIC SO THAT EVERYONE IN THE NEW LAND CAN WITNESS THE NEXT STEP.

OUR WORLD WAS UNDER ATTACK...

... BY A REALM MADE JUST FOR ME.

MY FATHER HAD CODED A SAFE HAVEN....

... NOW THAT HAVEN WAS SET TO CREATE HELL.

JUST THEN, ALL AROUND ME, FEAR AND TERROR STRUCK HOME.

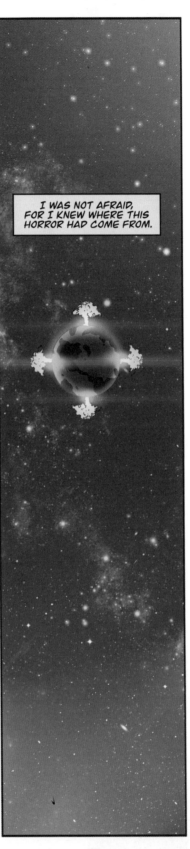

I WAS NOT AFRAID, FOR I KNEW WHERE THIS HORROR HAD COME FROM.

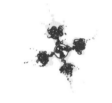

BUT I FELT AS HELPLESS AS EVERYONE ELSE...

JUST LOOK AT WHAT *I'VE* DONE!

D'YOU THINK KNOX KNOWS THAT I'M THE ONE WHO PUT HIS PLAN INTO ACTION?

ARLO, SHUT THIS DOWN! JUST MAKE IT STOP!

CORE COMPONEN

Energy Taps

Flow Vent

Surge Control

Current R action: Gateway

WE'VE HARDLY STARTED....

Surge Control

Stall

Hold

Accelerate

Overdrive

I'M HOPING THE BEST HAS YET TO COME!

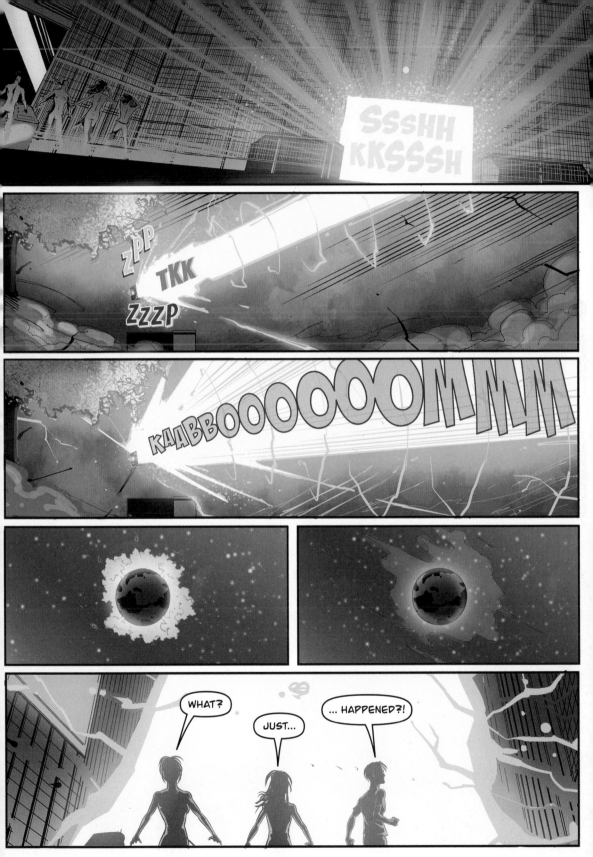

95

SOMETHING ABOUT A SHOWER.

A SHOWER?

SHE'S GOING TO TAKE A SHOWER?

LISTEN TO HER WITH ACCESS TO HOT WATER! IS THAT A MILITARY PERK?

GUYS, I'M SURE SHE'S NOT TALKING ABOUT PERSONAL HYGIENE HERE.

LET'S JUST HOPE THAT SOMEONE HAS A PLAN.

IT'S BEEN SO LONG SINCE I TOOK A SELFIE, THAT I CAN'T REMEMBER WHAT I LOOK LIKE IN A GOOD LIGHT.

LOOKING GOOD, LIONEL. MAL... IT'S BEEN A WHILE. ALL OK, I HOPE.

EVERYTHING IS **GREAT!** APART FROM, Y'KNOW... OUR RETURN TO THE DARK AGES.

I JUST HOPE THESE GUYS ARE ON TOP OF THINGS. WE ALL KNOW THAT E.SCAPE IS BEHIND THIS BUT HAVE YOU TRIED TO TELL THEM?

OH, SEVERAL TIMES.

AT THE LAST ATTEMPT, THE PRIME MINISTER'S SECURITY TEAM THREATENED TO HAVE ME PROSECUTED FOR HARASSING HIM.

WHAT? LIKE A STALKING CHARGE?

... MORE LIKE A WEIRDO ALERT.

YES, I DO KNOW HOW CREEPY THAT SOUNDS! BUT AT LEAST I TRIED.

WHAT ELSE CAN WE DO? THIS ISN'T ABOUT ME. IT'S ABOUT OUR WORLD!

105

JASPAR, THAT'S THE MOST GENUINE THING YOU'VE EVER SAID TO ME. THANKS FOR REACHING OUT.

I'M JUST TRYING TO DO THE RIGHT THING, MAL. AND THAT EXTENDS TO NOT GIVING UP ON EVIE. SOMEONE HAS TO GET THROUGH TO HER.

SOMEONE SHE RESPECTS, WHO HAS A WAY WITH WORDS... A GUY WHO'S GENUINE AND CARING...

OH, DON'T START. YOU WERE DOING SO WELL.

ACTUALLY, I WAS THINKING LIONEL IS OUR MAN.

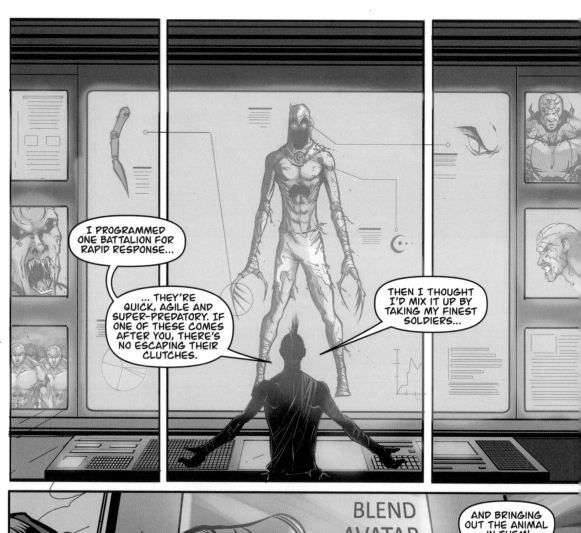

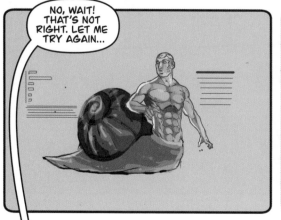

NO WAY, LIONEL! I'M DONE WITH E.SCAPE. WE'RE THROUGH!

JUST TAKE YOUR LAPTOP TO THE AUTHORITIES, EVIE. SHOW THEM THE APP.

EXPLAIN WHAT YOUR DAD CREATED HERE, SO THEY CAN FIGURE OUT A WAY TO PULL THE PLUG!

SAY NOTHING AND THEY PLAN TO BLOW UP THE PORTALS!

THAT WOULD BE A BAD IDEA.

I KNOW! WHICH IS WHY YOU HAVE TO TALK TO THE PEOPLE IN CHARGE!

DON'T DO IT FOR ME, EVIE.

DO IT FOR EVERYONE WHO CONSIDERS THIS WORLD TO BE HOME!

I'M SORRY, LIONEL.

IT'S OVER FOR ME.

WELL, THIS ISN'T EVIE'S LAPTOP.

HEY, THEY'RE HERE! PEOPLE, IT'S HAPPENING!

LET'S JUST GET OUT OF HERE...

THE MILITARY HAVE THIS PLACE ON LOCKDOWN, BUT IT'S VITAL WE REACH EVIE BEFORE--

TARGET DOWN. STILL GOT A LIVE ONE...

RIVER!! NOOO!

FREEZE! PUT YOUR HANDS IN THE AIR!

YOU MIGHT WANT TO LOOK AWAY, MA'AM. THIS IS GONNA HIT THEM HARD!

MARK MY WORDS, ARLO, YOUR ACTIONS WILL COME BACK TO HAUNT YOU.

I MIGHT'VE LEFT THAT WORLD LONG AGO, BUT IT'S HOME TO REAL PEOPLE -- INCLUDING MY FLESH AND BLOOD!

YOU'VE HIJACKED A VIRTUAL PARADISE, CREATED FOR EVIE BY HER FATHER, AND TURNED IT INTO A SERIOUS THREAT TO HER WAY OF LIFE. NOW YOU MIGHT HAVE HER MOTHER IN CHAINS HERE, BUT SHE POSSESSES MY WARRIOR SPIRIT AS MUCH AS HER DAD'S COMMITMENT TO DOING THE RIGHT THING.

IF YOU WANT TO SEE HOW THAT COMES TOGETHER, THEN GO AHEAD AND PRESS THE BUTTON.

IF YOU'VE FINISHED...

... THEN LET THE UPRISING BEGIN!

BLINK BLINK BLINK BLINK BLINK BLINK

WHAT THE--?

PRIME MINISTER, I'M ASSUMING CONTROL HERE. ON MY WORD, IF IT MOVES...

... THEN TAKE IT DOWN!

BLINK BLINK BLINK

LOOK LIVELY, SOLDIERS. THE PM AND COLONEL SALT HAVE ARRIVED FOR THE BRIEFING

YOU GUYS BETTER HAVE A GOOD REASON WHY TWO TARGETS GOT AWAY.

MA'AM, WITH RESPECT, THAT PAIR ARE THE LEAST OF OUR WORRIES NOW.

BLINK

BLINK

BLINK

GRAGGGHHH!!!

ALL THOSE PEOPLE... ARLO, THIS IS WICKED!

TOTALLY WICKED...

OH. YOU MEAN NOT IN A GOOD WAY, RIGHT?

WELL, FRANKLY I'M SICK OF HEARING WHAT YOU THINK. YOUR TIME HAS BEEN AND GONE.

OH, AND BY THE WAY, WHEN I SAID I'D GO EASY ON YOUR DAUGHTER IF YOU HELPED ME OUT...

YOU TRAITOROUS LITTLE...

NOW, THAT'S NO WAY TO TALK TO THE BOY WHO BROUGHT A WHOLE WORLD TO ITS KNEES, IS IT? KNOX MIGHT'VE STARTED THIS, BUT I'M THE ONE WHO GOT THE JOB DONE.

WHEN THE DUST SETTLES, YOU'LL BE LOOKING AT *THE SUPREME LEADER!*

MY FEET! NOBODY TOLD ME THAT THE UNDERGROUND LEVELS IN YOUR WORLD WOULD BE SO FILTHY.

UNITY... NOT NOW.

132

GIVE ME A CHANCE TO REACH THAT GATEWAY AND I'LL SHUT DOWN THIS ATTACK!

GATEWAY? EVERY ATTEMPT WE'VE MADE TO PASS THROUGH IT HAS ENDED IN FAILURE.

PRIME MINISTER, THESE KIDS NEED TO RUN FOR THEIR LIVES LIKE EVERYONE ELSE! THEY'RE WASTING OUR TIME--

BUT IT LEADS TO A SPECIAL CREATION! E.SCAPE IS A VIRTUAL WORLD CREATED BY MY FATHER ESPECIALLY FOR ME.

IT'S TRUE, SIR. I'VE SEEN EVIE TRAVEL THERE IN THE BLINK OF AN EYE.

OH, COME ON! ARREST THESE IDIOTS AND FOCUS ON THE FIGHT!

WAIT!

SALT, INSTRUCT YOUR SOLDIERS TO LAY DOWN FIRE FOR THIS GIRL AND HER FRIENDS.

BUT YOU CAN'T JUST TRUST SOME RANDOM STRANGER AT THIS TIME!

IF SHE REALLY CAN MAKE IT THROUGH THE GATEWAY, I'M PREPARED TO GIVE HER A CHANCE.

!!!

WITH RESPECT, *SIR*, YOU'RE CHOOSING SOME KID'S FANTASY HERO MOMENT OVER THE CHANCE TO BLOW THAT TRANSPORTATION DEVICE TO SMITHEREENS! AT LEAST THEN WE CAN BEGIN TO ROUND 'EM UP!

THE ENEMY HAS HIT US HARD. WE CAN'T AFFORD TO TAKE CHANCES!

E.SCAPE IS PROGRAMMED TO REFLECT AND ENHANCE HUMAN BEHAVIOUR. ANY MISSILE STRIKE ON THAT GATEWAY WILL LITERALLY BLOW UP IN OUR FACES!

IT COULD EVEN TAKE OUT THE WHOLE WORLD!

HOW LONG DO YOU NEED TO SHUT THIS THING DOWN?

LESS THAN YOU THINK. TIME MOVES FAST IN E.SCAPE.

THEN WE SHOULD ENGAGE THE MISSILE LAUNCH PROCEDURE RIGHT NOW, SIR! IF SHE'S NOT BACK ONCE THE WARHEAD'S COOKING ON COUNTDOWN, THAT'S TOO BAD.

DO WE HAVE A DEAL, EVIE?

DEAL, SIR!

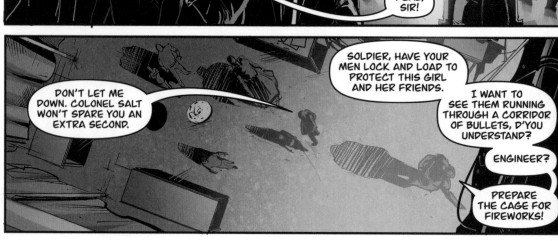

DON'T LET ME DOWN. COLONEL SALT WON'T SPARE YOU AN EXTRA SECOND.

SOLDIER, HAVE YOUR MEN LOCK AND LOAD TO PROTECT THIS GIRL AND HER FRIENDS.

I WANT TO SEE THEM RUNNING THROUGH A CORRIDOR OF BULLETS, D'YOU UNDERSTAND?

ENGINEER?

PREPARE THE CAGE FOR FIREWORKS!

ARE YOU GOING TO STAND BY AND WATCH AS SHE MAKES A RUN ACROSS THE SQUARE?

EVEN IF THE GATEWAY WON'T OPEN FOR US, THAT'S NO WAY FOR HEROES TO BEHAVE.

??

OK, I'M IN!

YOU *ARE?*

OH. WELL, OBVIOUSLY I'LL BE RIGHT BY YOUR SIDE... OR JUST BEHIND YOU.

WHATEVER WORKS... Y'KNOW?

GUYS, IF THERE'S ONE THING E.SCAPE HAS TAUGHT ME, IT'S THIS:

NO MATTER WHAT HAPPENS FROM HERE ON OUT, I'M NEVER TRULY ALONE. EVEN IF WE'RE WORLDS APART, YOU'RE RIGHT HERE WITH ME.

NOW LET'S KICK SOME VIRTUAL BUTT!

GRACHHH

PART THREE

YOU KNOW THAT KICK YOU GET WHEN A WHOLE WORLD FALLS TO ITS KNEES AND YOU'RE RESPONSIBLE?

YEAH, THAT!

A BIGGER MAN THAN YOU WOULD END THIS TORMENT, ARLO.

WELL, I'M SET TO DO JUST THAT...

THESE BRUTES ARE BADASS, RIGHT? WELL, THERE'S JUST ENOUGH JUICE LEFT IN THE BATTERY CORE TO MAKE THE LAST OF THEM...

SUPERSIZED!

GET THAT MISSILE CAGE PRIMED ON THE DOUBLE!

ON IT, SIR!

BLINK

BLINK

BLINK

BLINK

BLINK

BLINK

BLINK

WHAT IS THAT THING?

PRIME MINISTER, WE'RE IN TROUBLE...

TRUST DAD TO INSTALL A SECRET BACKDOOR.

A MASTER CODER IN BODY AND SOUL!

NOW KEEP YOUR VOICE DOWN, WE'RE ALMOST THERE...

PEOPLE, I'VE GATHERED YOU HERE TO WITNESS THE FINAL SPECTACLE! ONCE THE BATTERY CORE LEVELS ARE RECHARGED...

... I'M GONNA UNLEASH A SUPERBRUTE SO BIG IT'LL STRIDE BETWEEN CONTINENTS!

LET ME GO!

OH, BE QUIET AND WATCH THE OLD WORLD FALL!

SHHH!

UNITY, WHAT YOU'RE ABOUT TO WITNESS WON'T BE PRETTY.

EVIE, I MUST ASK YOU TO BE CAREFUL...

NO TIME!

I GOTTA SAY I WOULDN'T WANT TO BE KNOX RIGHT NOW.

THAT PLANET MUST BE FALLING APART ALL AROUND HIS EARS!

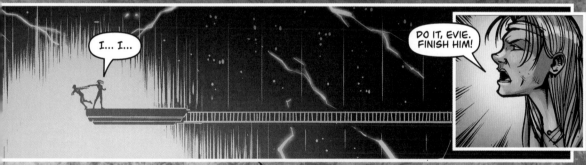

READY FOR THIS?

BRING IT ON!

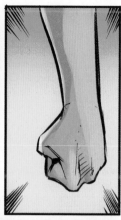

DON'T MESS WITH A MOTHER AND HER DAUGHTER!

—HUH?

WE'LL OUTWIT YOU. EVERY TIME!

KRAK

WHAT WOULD DAD SAY IF HE COULD SEE US NOW?

HE WOULDN'T SAY A WORD, MY LOVE.

PRIDE GOES BEYOND WORDS.

EVIE, YOUR WORLD IS ON THE BRINK...

... OF BECOMING HISTORY!

AT LAST, IT SEEMS WE AGREE ON SOMETHING!

YOU'RE A SPIRITED SOUL, EVIE. I'LL GIVE YOU THAT. JUST THINK, IF THINGS HAD WORKED OUT DIFFERENTLY, YOU COULD'VE BEEN MY RIGHT HAND WOMAN.

DREAM ON, LOSER!

THIS ISN'T OVER YET! WHILE MY FRIENDS ARE STILL ALIVE, YOU CAN BE SURE THEY'RE LOOKING OUT FOR ME!

WHAP

AND EVEN WITH MY DYING BREATH, I'LL NEVER GIVE UP ON THEM!

GRAAGHHH!!

WE'RE ALMOST OUT OF AMMO.

SARGE, IT'S TIME TO RETREAT!

NOWHERE TO GO, SOLDIER! *STAY FROSTY!*

STAY FROSTY? WHAT DO THEY THINK THIS IS?! A VIDEOGAME?

THEY'RE NOT FOOLING AROUND, JASPAR...

CHECK IT OUT!

MA'AM, ALL WARHEADS ARE NOW WIRED AND LIVE.

THEN DROP THAT CAGE AND COMMENCE COUNTDOWN! TEAM EARTH JUST GOT *TEETH!*

HOW FAR SHOULD WE GO FOR A LIFELONG FRIEND?

JUST THEN, UNITY SHOWED ME THE WAY.

KKSSHHHH

IN THAT MOMENT, I SAW THE LIGHT...

HHHSSSKK

BAKAAM

AND I KNEW WHAT HAD TO BE DONE.

THE SYSTEM'S STILL LIVE! UNITY'S SACRIFICE DIDN'T CRASH IT!

MUM, IT'S GOING TO TAKE MORE THAN AN AVATAR TO FINISH THIS.

?!?

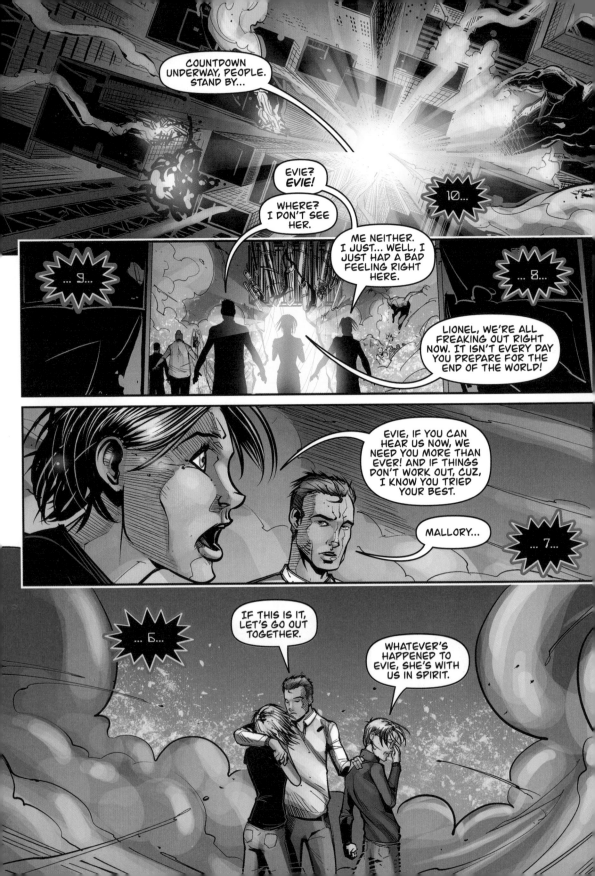

EVIE, MY LOVE! PLEASE DON'T DO THIS. THERE HAS TO BE ANOTHER WAY!

DON'T MAKE ME TURN AROUND, MUM. IT'S TOO HARD...

?!

WAKE UP, IDIOTS! STOP HER BEFORE SHE DESTROYS US ALL!

YOU WILL DO NO SUCH THING...

OOF!

... EVEN THOUGH IT BREAKS MY HEART TO BE A PART OF THIS.

AND SO I HAD MY MOTHER'S BLESSING, WHICH MEANT SO MUCH TO ME.

IT MEANT I DIDN'T FEEL ALONE AS I PREPARED TO STEP INTO THE UNKNOWN, HOPING IT WOULD SAVE MY WORLD.

I WAS WITH FAMILY.

AND AMONG FRIENDS.

IN A PLACE THAT WAS ALWAYS DESIGNED FOR ME TO FEEL AT PEACE.

169

... ONE FORMED OF MEMORIES HELD BY THOSE WHO SHARED MY LIFE...

... A REALM OF LOVE...

... AND LIGHT.

PARADISE IS RIGHT HERE. IT EXISTS FOR EVERY ONE OF US.

ALL WE HAVE TO DO IS OPEN OUR EYES TO WHAT WE STAND TO LOSE, AND PROTECT IT WITH OUR LIVES.

MY FATHER HAD SET OUT TO CREATE A DIGITAL PARADISE... IN DOING SO, HE LOST SIGHT OF THE REAL THING.

IN CRASHING HIS CREATION, I KNOW DAD UNDERSTANDS THAT I DID THE RIGHT THING.

FOR WE'RE TOGETHER AS A FAMILY AT LAST.

NOW AND FOREVERMORE.

... TO REMEMBER A TRUE HEROINE WHO MADE THE ULTIMATE SACRIFICE FOR US ALL...

... AND HAS EARNED HER PLACE IN HISTORY AS THE GIRL WHO SAVED THE WORLD.

EVIE

Daughter, Friend, Warrior.

SPEAKING TO THOSE WHO KNEW HER BEST, I'VE LEARNED HOW EVIE STRIVED TO DO THE RIGHT THING – EVEN WHEN SHE DOUBTED HER ABILITIES – AND THAT SHOULD BE A LESSON TO US ALL.

SO, AS WE PICK UP THE PIECES OF OUR LIVES, LET US FOLLOW EVIE'S EXAMPLE.

LOOK OUT FOR EACH OTHER, PEOPLE. BE PREPARED TO GO THE DISTANCE FOR THOSE IN NEED -- EVEN IF IT REQUIRES A LEAP OF FAITH.

WITH THIS IN MIND, I HAVE BEEN CONSIDERING THE CASE OF COLONEL SALT...

... WHO FACES MULTIPLE CHARGES FOR HER CONDUCT DURING THE UPRISING.

YES, SHE CAME CLOSE TO WIPING US OUT BY OUR OWN HAND, BUT I MUST LOOK BEYOND HER ACTIONS AND FOCUS ON HER MOTIVES.

AT HEART, SHE WAS TRYING TO PROTECT US...

... AND FOR THIS REASON, I AM PARDONING HER.

NATURALLY, I'LL MISS MY FRIENDS. I JUST TAKE COMFORT FROM THE FACT THAT THEY'LL MOVE ON FROM THIS MOMENT.

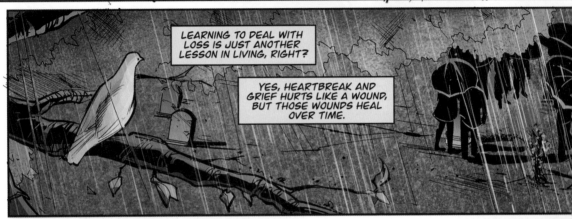

LEARNING TO DEAL WITH LOSS IS JUST ANOTHER LESSON IN LIVING, RIGHT?

YES, HEARTBREAK AND GRIEF HURTS LIKE A WOUND, BUT THOSE WOUNDS HEAL OVER TIME.

THAT'S WHEN YOU CAN FACE AN EX WITHOUT STRINGS...

... OR REFLECT ON THE DEPARTED WITHOUT EYES BRIGHT WITH TEARS.

Daughter, Friend, Warrior.

AS FOR THE SCARS, OFTEN THEY MARK THE FACT THAT WE OVERCAME ADVERSITY BY REACHING OUT TO THOSE WHO CARE FOR US...

... AND THOSE SCARS BECOME A PART OF OUR STORY...

... THEY BRING US CLOSER TO UNDERSTANDING OURSELVES...

YOUR PHONE STILL HAS SOME JUICE?

≥TSK≤ WHO WOULD BE MESSAGING YOU NOW, ALL YOUR FRIENDS ARE HERE.

♫ TRILL-I-LING TRILL-I-LING ♪

OH! SORRY! EXCUSE ME FOR A MOMENT...

... AND REMIND US OF SOMETHING WE SHOULD NEVER FORGET...

THANK YOUs

WELL... THERE YA HAVE IT! I HOPE YOU ENJOYED *USERNAME:UPRISING*. THIS IS THE THIRD THANK YOU PAGE I'VE WRITTEN AND I'M CONSCIOUS OF REPEATING THE SAME THING FOR THE THIRD YEAR IN A ROW, SO I'LL TRY AND KEEP IT SHORTER AND SWEETER.

I WANT TO SAY A MASSIVE THANK YOU TO YOU ALL FOR YOUR UNBEATABLE SUPPORT THROUGHOUT THE USERNAME TRILOGY. IT HONESTLY HAS BEEN LIFE-CHANGING FOR ME AND WOULDN'T HAVE BEEN POSSIBLE WITHOUT YOU.

THANK YOU SO MUCH TO BRIONY AND THE REST OF TEAM HODDER! YOU HAVE BEEN INCREDIBLE FROM START TO FINISH, WITH BOOK STUFF AND JUST BEING LEGENDS IN GENERAL.

ONCE AGAIN, MASSIVE THANK YOU TO THE SUGG SQUAD: AMRIT, MATT, JOAQUIN AND MINDY. I'M HONESTLY SO PLEASED WITH HOW THIS BOOK -- ALONG WITH THE PREVIOUS TWO -- HAS TURNED OUT. IT'S BEEN AN HONOUR TO WORK WITH YOU ALL FOR THE PAST THREE YEARS AND I HOPE WE WILL CROSS PATHS AGAIN IN THE FUTURE AND CREATE THE NEXT BIG GRAPHIC NOVEL SERIES!

SHOUT OUT TO ALEX, ZARA, LUCY AND JOSH D FOR WORKING SO HARD
ALONGSIDE ME TO MAKE THIS BOOK SO GREAT. THE 24 HOUR LIVE
SHOW WAS A REAL TEST FOR US ALL BUT I WAS SO PROUD OF HOW
YOU HELPED ME STAY AWAKE AND GAVE ME THE SUPPORT I NEEDED
THROUGHOUT THE WHOLE PROCESS.

LASTLY THANKS TO MY FAMILY AND FRIENDS. IT CAN BE GOOD TO
BE SURROUNDED BY 'YES' PEOPLE IN YOUR LIFE WHO TELL YOU
EVERYTHING YOU DO IS A GOOD IDEA ETC., BUT IT'S MORE IMPORTANT
TO HAVE PEOPLE IN YOUR LIFE WHO ARE TOTALLY HONEST WITH YOU
AND WHO AREN'T AFRAID TO TELL YOU WHEN SOMETHING ISN'T GREAT.
I FEEL LIKE I'VE GROWN UP WITH THE PERFECT BALANCE OF THOSE
PEOPLE AND FOR THAT I AM VERY GRATEFUL. THANK YOU ALL FOR
HELPING ME BECOME THE PERSON I AM TODAY.

JOE X

P.S I RECKON I COULD DOWN A HALF PINT NOW.